The Scientific Invention of Hieroglypns

or

Hurrah for Pliny!

Rosalind Park
with
Illustrations by Valerie Matthews

Azoth Publications
1997

Copyright © 1997, R. Park.

ISBN No. 0 9532056 0 6

Published by Azoth Publications, 19 Kings Road, Westcliff-on-Sea, Essex SS0 8LL
Printed in Great Britain by S.O.S., Leigh-on-Sea, Essex

For

Joy

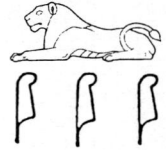

The greatest Mother on Earth

Egypt is a place of wonder and mystery. The above photograph replicates a vision I had on the North face of the Pyramid of Khufu (see page 25) as seen from my balcony room at the Mena House Hotel, during my maiden visit in September 1985.

Wherever we have spoken openly, we have said nothing.
But where we have written something in code and in
pictures, we have concealed the Truth.

Rosarium philosophorum
Circa. 13th Century

Contents

Introduction	1
Myth and Political Correctness	5
Early Philosophers	6
Egyptian Enquiry into Nature	8
Ancient Science, Hidden Cosmology	13
Thoth Rules, Okay?	21
Ra is Supreme	26
Loose Ends	32
Selective Bibliography	38

INTRODUCTION

> *I have arranged together many and astonishing things from the ancients, which have the power to persuade those who read them, repeating that the ancients set forth many teachings which are hard to solve and enigmatical.*
>
> Vettius Valens, *The Anthology Book VI*
> 2nd Century AD

Old Kingdom Natural Philosophy

The traditional notion is that any well-reasoned Natural History and Science, loosely termed 'the enquiry into nature', was first espoused by the Greeks. I take an unfashionable view that the Old Kingdom's priestly caste (with their identical intellectual apparatus) had already deduced much the same. Their version of Natural Philosophy merely had modifications to suit the culture, environment and technology of the respective times. The split-hairs difference in Science anachronisms of Greeks verses Egyptians is because there is no apparent literature available to us of Ancient Egyptian scientific thought.

All great thinkers need exercises to challenge the mind. To the perceptive individual, counting and measuring all that surrounded him were a means of understanding the basic components of life. Erik Iversen, the Danish Egyptologist, acknowledges that the Ancient Egyptians had as much in mental facilities for empirical observation as the Greeks or us. However, he puts the difference down to the Egyptians having "an entirely different conception of the dynamic process of the cosmos". He further felt a "peculiarity of Egyptian thought" was the reluctance to use abstract concepts and the "dependence on concrete mythical representations to express a theoretical conception of the nature of things". Iversen gives as an example the notion that phenomena such as celestial bodies and their movements could only be given in mythical terms, without any conception of their true nature. Even coming from the bias of egyptological scholarship, Iversen (1993) sums up as follows: *"all Egyptian reasoning . . . left no possibility open for the development of an independent logic and an empirical science in our sense of the words. The truth throughout the whole history of Egyptian thought was never, as with the Greeks and ourselves, a scientific or philosophical, based on empirical observations and logic deductions".*

Language of Ancient Egypt

Much has already been written on the language of Ancient Egypt since its decipherment in the 19th century. Sophisticated studies continue to be done. The ancient Egyptians had an elegant and meaning-laden system primarily of stone-carved communication (*medu netcher* = "the god's words"). Complicated linguistics may now be leading us away from the mind, heart and skeletal beauty of a language meant for the king on earth and the gods in heaven. Some of the essential hieroglyphs form a numerical and word/picture configuration, which aptly describes the physical world of the early Nile dwellers. They are also representative of the elementary sciences of their culture.

In our day and age, there still exists a wide-gap polarity between the societies using space-age technology to the rare groups, who (by virtue of isolation or race) rely on the stone-age tools of their forebears. Human sociobiologists are unable to tell us whether the cultural differences are determined by environmental or genetic factors; and those foolish to argue even a liberal case of racial differences enter an area of academic booby traps and landmines.

In my view, the phonetic function of the signs has been over-emphasised by scholars of Egyptian language. The rebus writing of Egyptian pictograms *did* represent perceptions as well as objects.

Written music is another form of notation, and as Victor Hugo reminds us: "when a musician <u>reads</u> a score, he <u>hears</u> it". Academic dyslexia (word blindness/deafness) on my part inclined me to ignore the sound value, and ask **why** such particular images were chosen in the first place.

System or Accident

Were the original hieroglyphs a few disparate images put together in a muddle by a bunch of shaman drawing in the sand and playing "I-spy-with-my-little-eye", or something unique deliberated upon by the intellectual elite of the Nile valley? Anyone who correctly draws hieroglyphs becomes aware of underlying micro mathematics in the master design. The symbols were created with intended precision on an invisible square grid pattern, each to align in harmony and compliment the other. For me, the hieroglyphs also project some quintessence or stereotype of Ancient Egypt's unique psychology. They do it not only by virtue of gracious charm but also by a "childish" picture writing that cannot abandon the characteristic traits of obsessive neatness, rigid attitude and an inflexible mode of expression, which operates within self imposed claustrophobic boundaries.

In writing on the origins of hierogylphs, Henry G. Fisher (1989) describes the hypothetical inventor of Egyptian writing as "a talented draftsman".

HIEROGLYPHS 2600 BC

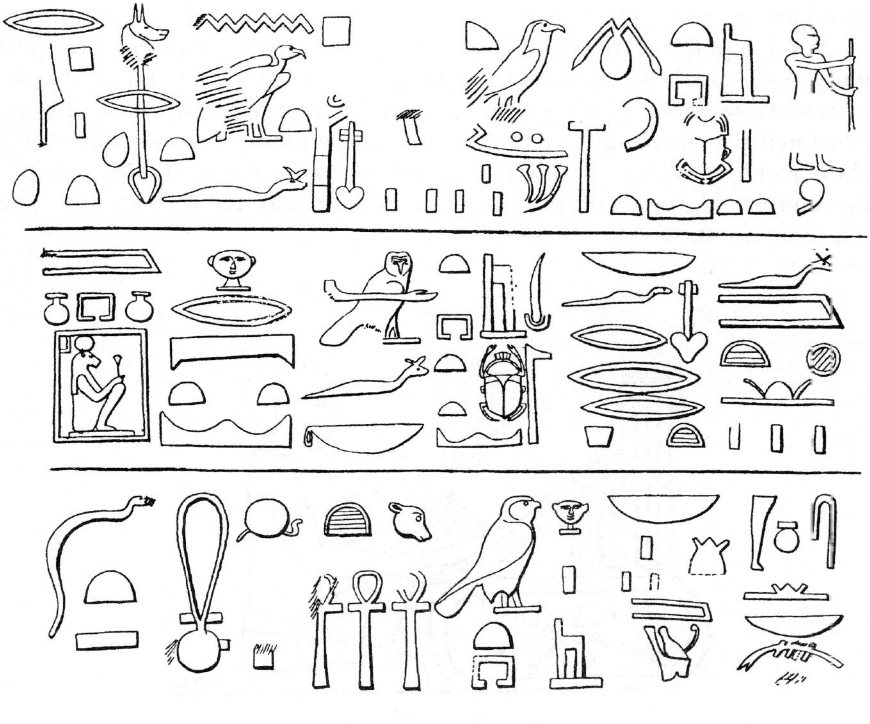

HIEROGLYPHS APPROX. 75 BC

In a reappraisal of how the hieroglyphs might have come about, one needs to look more critically at <u>and</u> beyond the face-value of the actual symbols. The conundrum of *picture-writing-which-isn't*, hints tantalisingly to me at a sophisticated process of mental abstraction in the compilers who assembled the Egyptian language in the 3rd millennium BC or long before for all anyone can say with certainty.

Proto-hieroglyphs

Sir William Flinders Petrie (1912) was of the opinion that there was some common and widely used system long before historic Egyptian 'civilisation'. He based this on his findings of potters' marks on Neolithic pottery that mimicked the later hieroglyphs.. Working from hieroglyphs of royal names on tags and sealings of Dynasty 0, scholars today believe that early (around 3200 BC) writing developed in Egypt to serve the state. The southern Egyptian tomb "U-j", (in a site excavated by Günter Dreyer in a sector overlooked by Petrie) at the Abydos necropolis of the first kings, contained large quantities of Egyptian, *and* Palestinian, pottery together with 125 bone labels. The latter artifacts are inscribed with many indecipherable signs, that nevertheless appear to be the prototypes of hieroglyphs.

Was it a panel of inventors or a single genius from within the group who actually gave birth to Egyptian writing? We shall never know. Modern investigators seem to have assumed that the hieroglyphs were simple two-dimensional flat drawings to be read on a single plane. Is it possible that the symbols would have been understood by the earliest scribes and priests, as being isometric shapes, with plumped-up volume, and that they had the ability to rotate on an axis?

MYTH AND POLITICAL CORRECTNESS

The Greeks created thought?

Writing in 1951, that centenarian Egyptologist, Margaret Murray believed "the Greeks are responsible for many of the modern ideas concerning the Egyptian system of writing. With their genius for misunderstanding anything outside the narrow limits of their own small country, they ascribed mystical meanings to a script they could not read, and gazed with awe at the strange signs sculptured on temples and tombstones".

In 1993, the venerable Iversen (already quoted above) wrote in a new preface to his 1961 work, "any talk of an Egyptian influence on Greece was considered not merely heretical, but almost sacrilegious, a vain infringement on the pristine purity of Greek thought". Like Murray, Iversen believes that when the entire system of hieroglyphic writing was forgotten in Classical times, what survived was "the completely wrong but most fertile myth about the hieroglyphs as a sacred writing of ideas".

This myth pervades the minds of the academics. Possibly some confusion about concrete and abstract ideas were hard to grasp in antiquity just as theoretical physics concepts are for the average person today. Carl Jung believed contemporary man to be blind to the facts and that, with all his rationality and efficiency, believes he is possessed by "powers" that are beyond his control. As Wittgenstein says: "There are indeed things that cannot be put into words. They make themselves manifest. They are what is mystical" (Proposition 6.522); and "It is not how things are in the world that is mystical, but that it exists" (Proposition 6.44).

EARLY PHILOSOPHERS

> *Having assigned boundaries to its space, we restitute the place's own Truth.*
>
> De arte Mensoria 1
> Frontinus (35-103 AD)

The poetic metaphor from the 19th Dynasty Chester Beatty papyrus: "Do not turn your back on *hieroglyphs* (Lesko, 1994) or you shall be thoroughly beaten", might be taken two ways. Firstly as an admonition to a recalcitrant learner scribe, and secondly as yet another traditional wise saying of which the Ancient Egyptians were so fond.

By the 19th Dynasty, according to Iversen (1993), decline had begun. The origin of various signs had been forgotten, there was confusion over their use, and over attempts to improve on the established word pictures.

While not quoting any particular Egyptian case, Diodorus Siculus believed that the earliest generations had developed their conventional and symbolic type of writing by "agreeing with one another upon symbols for each thing which was to be attached to each term" (1.7.6-8.4). Further on he records Egyptian claims that certain inventions came from their gods (1.14.1-15.8), and that ancient controversy existed between one race and another over who were the first discoverers of things useful for life (1.9.3-2.38, & 4.1.6-2.5).

Clement of Alexandria (*Stromata*, 5.4.20-21) distinguished three types of Egyptian writing whose usage ranged from mundane to the holy. Those most revered, the hieroglyphs, described as "sacred carved letters" were of two kinds: "Of the symbolic, one kind speaks literally by imitation, and another writes as it were figuratively; and another is quite allegorical, using certain enigmas" (5.4.20).

For me, most accurate explanation, by far, of the ancient recognition of the hieroglyphs, comes from the amazing polymath Pliny (died heroically 79AD). When discussing the two obelisks in Rome, he gives us the simple statement of fact: the hieroglyphs comprised "an account of Natural Science according to the theories of the Egyptian sages" (Book XXXVI, 71-73). It was Pliny who gave the world of science a ranking classification, which was non-evolutionary in the Darwinian sense. This was his hierarchical view of Natural History taken in ascending order:

Universe
Earth
Human beings
Animals
Plants
Minerals

For Pythagoras, whom Pliny tells us was in Egypt during the reign of Psammetichus II (26th Dynasty circa 590BC), the basis of the universe was Number. Diogenes Laertius (VIII,3) reports that Pythagorus knew the Egyptian language.

It is remiss that so few enquiring minds in Greek and Roman science sought the rationale and esoteric meaning of the hieroglyphs. The Greeks had already established themselves in Egypt, at the Milesian City of Naukratis in the Delta, around 630BC. This was some 400 years before the famous decree of Ptolemy V, later found in the vicinity of nearby Rosetta. Whichever race he came from, behind the anonymous artisan who executed the Rosetta stone's 3 texts so beautifully was an expertly bilingual scribe. Furthermore, he must have had many equivalent peers to realise commissions for "every prominent temple in the land". We are led to believe that in five centuries, the only highborn Greek who bothered to learn the ancient Egyptian language was Cleopatra VII. It seems unlikely as the same class of Romans failing to know Greek.

In the 3rd Century AD, Plotinus (*Enneads* V, 8.6) speculated that the Egyptians had arrived at a method by means of which they could write with distinct pictures of material objects. To the initiated, they gave a profound insight into the very essence and substance of things – the neoplatonic myth of the hieroglyphs.

EGYPTIAN ENQUIRY INTO NATURE

And the Earth and the Water were separated, either from the other, as the logos *would; and the Earth brings forth from herself, such living creatures as she had, four-footed and creeping beasts, wild and tame.*

The Divine Pymander of
Hermes Mercurius Trismegistus
Doctor Everard (1650)

Metaphysics in Egypt

One way or another, Egypt guarded *science* well. Other than two written texts from a library of Epicurean philosophy at Herculaneum (Italy), all documents relating to Greek science have been recovered exclusively from Egypt. The earliest surviving Euclidean fragment of 225 BC came from Elephantine Island; while the earliest securely dated papyrus remains at 330 BC.

From the metaphysical theories by the so-called pre-Socratean philosophers, vital substances thought to constitute basic life forms were liquid plus solid: Water plus Earth. Ancient scientists believed that all matter comprised elements, of which there were four – Fire, Air, Water and Earth. The Physician Galen (129-216 AD) in *De plenitudine* 3 [VII, 525-8 K] wrote "The Stoics say Air and Fire make things (become) cohesive, while <u>Earth</u> and <u>Water</u> are (already) made cohesive". Early in the first millennium BC, and predating Empedocles, Chinese medicine incorporated the theories of Ying and Yang polarities, and also Elements of which they had an extra one of *wood*.

Thales was the earliest enquirer into the nature of things as a whole that we know about. A standing statue of him, next to a seated Pythagoras, is to be found amongst a semicircular group of Greek philosopher statues at Saqqara. This tribute was set up by Ptolemy I in front of a now ruined temple of Nectanebo II (circa 360-343 BC).

Born in 624 BC, Thales visited Naukratis as a trader-traveller before settling back in his native Miletus and gaining later fame as the Father of Greek Science. Proclus (*in Euclidem*) says that having practised philosophy in Egypt, Thales came to Miletus when he was older, as well as having brought the study of geometry out of Egypt to Greece. He believed that the world was essentially made of the element Water.

One may borrow some key concepts from the science-based standard model used far later by the Greeks and Romans namely:

> Number (Pythagoras)
> Animal, vegetable and mineral (Pliny)
> Water (Thales)
> Elements (Empedocles)

Hieroglyphs as representatives of the Elements

From the very beginning, the monoconsonantal signs were indispensable in writing words that could not otherwise be expressed. They also served to write some of the commonest words in the language. However, Iversen found it strange that merely with the invention of uniliteral signs, the Egyptians had already created the theoretical background for excluding all other graphic components. It would have been quite possible for them to discard all the extra elements by exclusive use of the unilaterals in a proper consonantic alphabet. Paradoxically however, "they never took this natural consequence of their own discoveries, but retained all the complexities of the original system throughout their history". Did they?

Although the hieroglyphs may have since lost their complex quality of wholeness by being liberated as simple free ranging individual *belle lettres*, one can perceive an original *schema*. It is possible to divide and sort the *basic matter* represented by the hieroglyphs in a letter by letter sequence into this design.

The monosonsonantal hieroglyphs (sometimes called the uniliteral signs), normally arranged for consideration according to the order of a Semitic alphabet like Arabic, are:

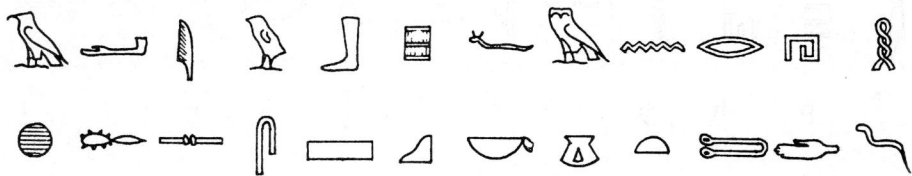

Elemental Water

As an aside, one might remark that the surviving artwork from the Old Kingdom tombs onward shows that the Egyptians were fascinated with taxonomy. Their astute, finely detailed versions of animal genera (**Species classification**) are particularly notable when recording the Aquatic (**Water**) World around them (see, for example, Brewer and Friedman 1989). In their spiritual beliefs too, the balance and imbalance, and stability and changeability of the Universe were fundamental concerns owing more to ancient rational "Science" than faith-based or magical "Religion".

The Hieroglyphs: a Species Classification

The first step is to separate these into life forms derived naturally from Water, and those solid or practical shapes, which could be made from the products of Earth.

The living 'Water' group ('Mother Nature' if you like) can easily be recognised in the signs for water, snakes, birds and anatomical glyphs:

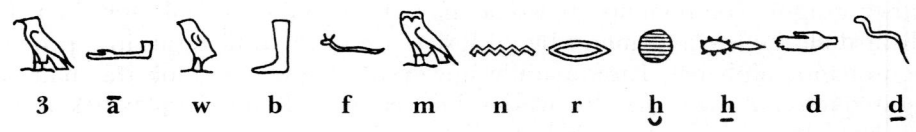

The less animate category derived from 'Earth' origins brought into being via technological intervention include the mountain or man-made mound, cultivated produce, and shelter together with manufactured products of everyday living:

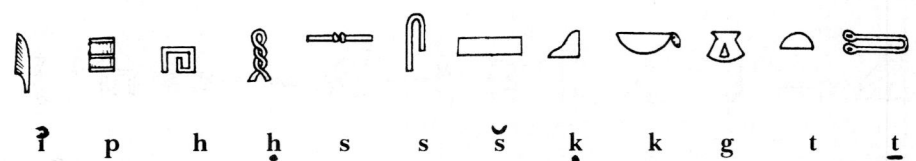

The next sorting is to assemble like things in numerical order, which automatically creates a separate category for individual species – 1 river, 2 snakes, 3 birds, 6 body parts representing the WATER group. When written down in hieroglyphic script, allowing a new line for each entity, a triangular flow of descending life forms in a Darwinian evolutionary order (i.e. Reptiles, Birds, and Mammals) is readily observed.

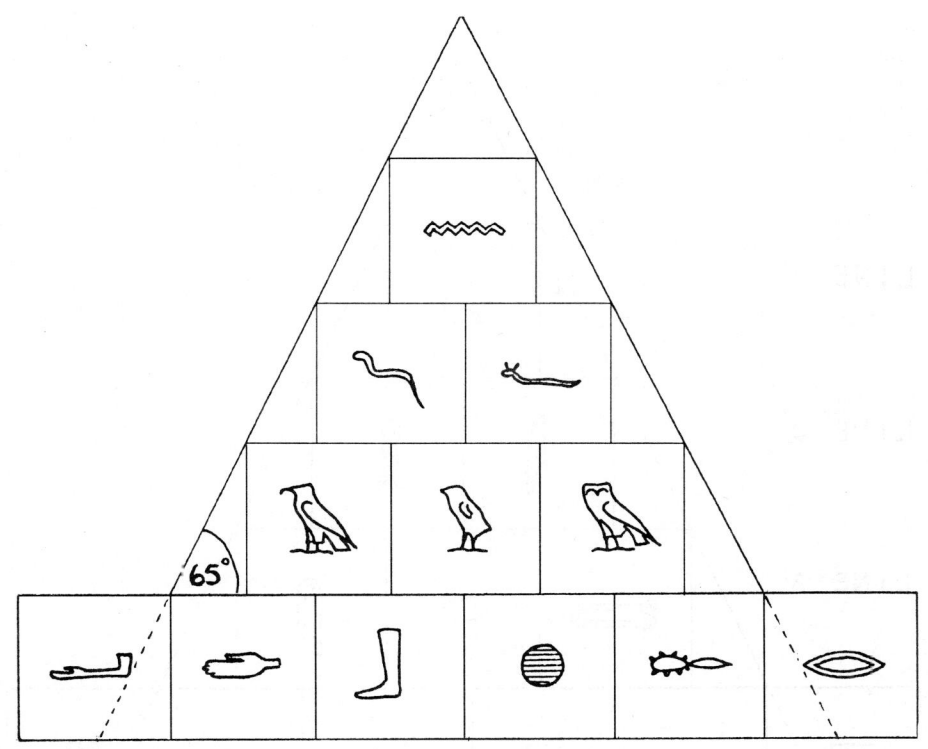

Having established that half the monoconsonantal hieroglyphs (my *Water* group) conform to a pattern, I look to the grouping of the remainder, symbols of the inanimate objects necessary for man's survival on earth.

This sorting reveals four categories: 1 hill, 2 botanicals. 2 items manufactured from crop materials, and 6 domestic items (I assume the *pool space* functions as an artificial reservoir or well). The descending order of EARTH commences at the mound (where trees grow or from which minerals are extracted). The next rank is the soil-grown plants that produce the cloth, bread and tethering rope. This follows on with products – a woven basket, hewn wood and/or stone products. Suspecting a running order, I have arranged my 4 lines in a logical guess: the *reed* on Line 2 connects to the *rope* on Line 3 which connects to the security of the home *reed shelter* and the *lock* on Line 4. The complementary flax on Line 2 links to the bolt of linen on Line 3, and further links to the weaving industry of *basket* and *stool*. The centre of Line 4 the water *jar-stand* pairs with the artificial *pool*!

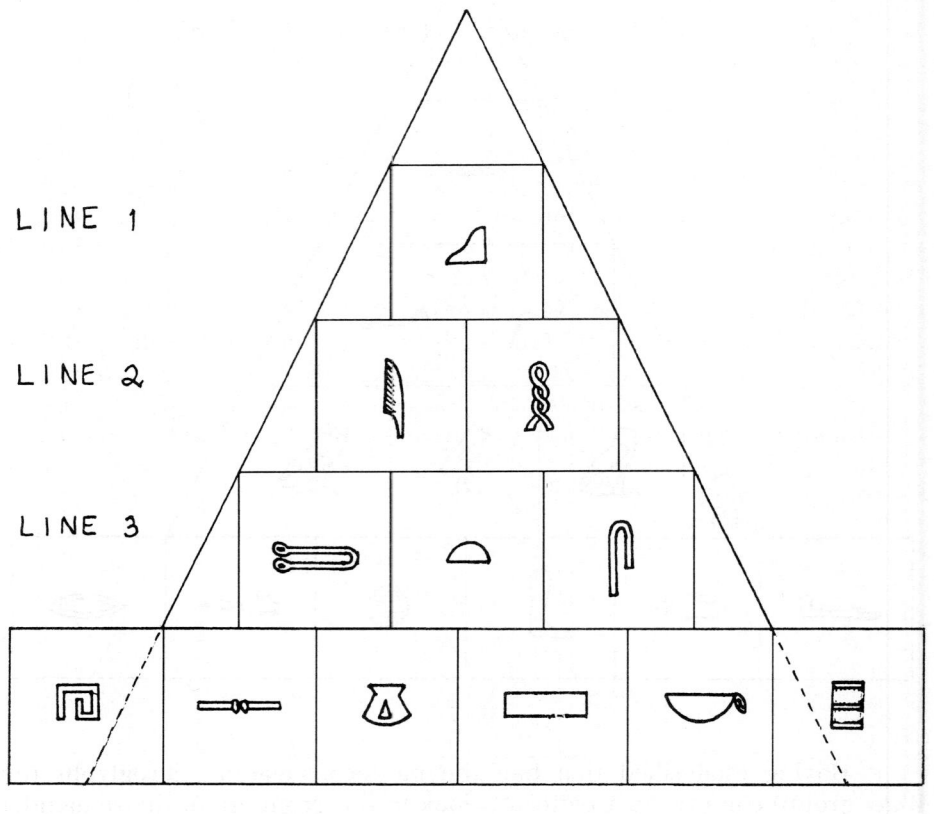

    The geometric arrangement of the letters, a triangle on top of a rectangle has created a secondary hieroglyph (*O* 24 in Gardiner's list) meaning "the pyramid".

This stacking arrangement of hieroglyphs in their invisible grid squares will produce slightly variable base angles depending upon the number of squares used per grid. A noteworthy feature is that four base letters (the *arm, mouth, shelter* and *stool*) remain outwith the triangle arrangements.

ANCIENT SCIENCE, HIDDEN COSMOLOGY

*Of wonders there are 3: god and man, mother and maid –
the 3 and the 1.*
M. Miier, 1618

At the beginning of my study, I split the alphabet and did a dissection of individual letters, which in an automatic order of natural progressions, reassembled each character into distinctive geometric shapes – an isosceles triangle (that made famous by Thales) resting on a rectangle. Keeping within the boundaries of original Old Kingdom geometry and Canon of Proportion, can the 24 hieroglyphs be regrouped into a cohesive assembly that will not be a meaningless random scatter? Amazingly the two triangles of Water and Earth figures are **chiral** forms of each other which I could twist on to each other in a mirror image. This procedure (made easier by images on acetate transparencies) gives a *three-dimensional* model. The flat *two-dimensional* picture (Figure 1) emerges as this juxtaposition looking like a design for snakes and ladders or a child's crossword puzzle:

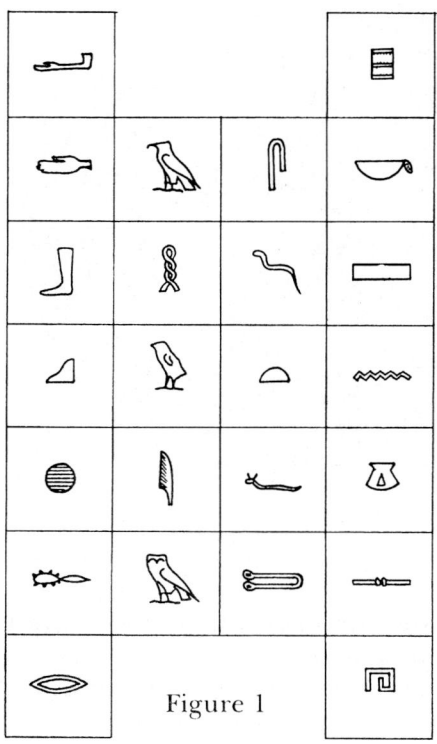

Figure 1

Playing Games

A child's game is not so ludicrous if you will allow me a slight digression. The evidence suggests that board games were greatly favoured for leisure activities, and at least six types were played in Ancient Egypt from Predynastic times. An Old Kingdom game was called *Mḥn* or "serpent". On display in the British Museum is a 2nd Dynasty game-board carved in pale yellow limestone that shows a snake curled around a central eye. According to the Pyramid Texts, *Mḥn* is the serpent-spirit who coils around the sun at midnight. Despite picture evidence on tombs and models recovered, there are no texts quoting rules on how the board games were actually meant to be played. A unique blueprint of the games *Mḥn* and *Snt* is painted on the wall of the tomb of Hesy-ra from the 3rd Dynasty. The erudite Hesy-ra (circa 2650 BC) is the first authenticated doctor in the world. He described himself as 'chief of dentists and doctors'. The game *Mḥn* is drawn as seven nested spirals-come-circles with grooved markings (Figure 2).

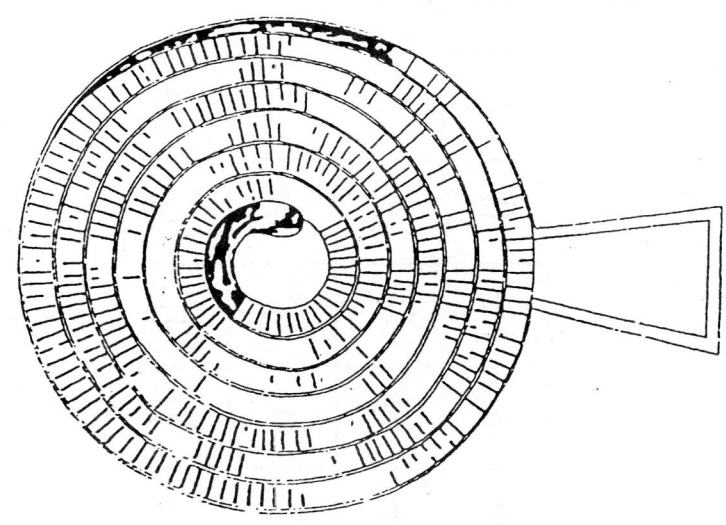

Figure 2

The crypto-crossword nucleus (Line 4 across of Fig. 1) contains 4 vital picture symbols of ancient scientific ideas. Would today's Classical Greek scholar, if he travelled back in time, be able to recognise 'science' if he actually saw it expressed other than in writing? I have already said that the *elements*

Earth and Water are represented by the hieroglyphs of the *mound* (or *hill*) and the letter "n" *water* sign. What of the other two hieroglyphs: the *quail-chick* and the semicircular *bread-loaf*? Do they occur by master design or by chance in the dead centre of the new format?

The letter "t" hieroglyph could be the allegorical 'bread of life'; its placement in Egyptian writing is used to signify Feminine gender. Not so easy, the letter "w", the *quail-chick* can be used to give plurity to words denoting gender – Masculine mostly.

| EARTH MASCULINE FEMININE WATER |

A Truth with a slight flaw: 3 + 1

Strictly speaking, I was in error when I went unscientifically in search of a letter that would fit the gender opposite feminine. Of the four central symbols – three concur with the argument, while one is slightly hybrid (or a misnomer in the classification system). A truth with a slight flaw is something one can observe in countless Egyptian art scenes. This has gone unrecorded by Egyptologists: the number Four expressed as **3 + 1**

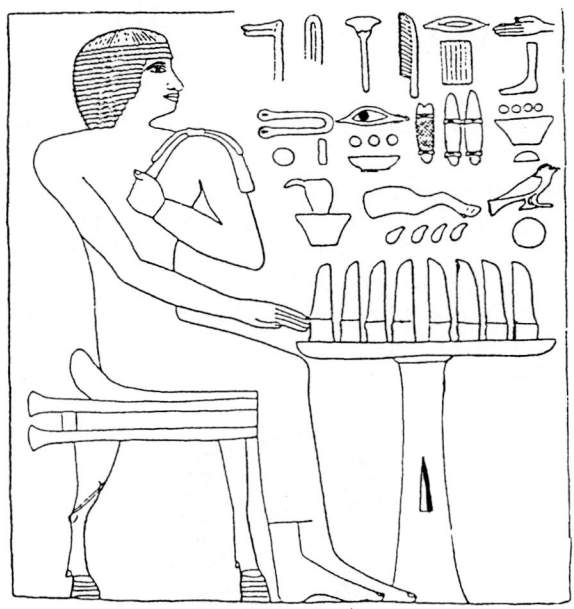

Fig. 3

A pertinent example can be seen on the elegant offering table of the 4th Dynasty high priest of Heliopolis, Rahotep who was also half-brother and Chief of Construction for the Pyramid of Khufu. The fine limestone funerary relief, unfortunately bereft of its beautiful colours due to none-too-careful archaeological squeeze technique on site at Meidum, is now in the British Museum. A partial line-drawing (Figure 3) on the upper register reveals distinct category offerings of **3** plant products plus **1** mineral items namely: figs, wine and incense from trees and vine, and various eye-paints ground from ores. The "animal" offering on the middle register of the offering table is represented as the foreleg of beef, which is also understood to be the constellation of Ursa Major in the directional flight path of the deceased soul to the Fields of Reeds (the next level). Prince Rahotep was also keen on games for included in his worldly goods inventory required for the next life were wooden furniture and **3** board games: *Mḥn*, *Snt* (hereafter called Senet), and *Mnt* ("endurance") a game on a slab with 13 panels.

Khufu's

Also from the Pyramid Age, the classic examples of this formula are the Canopic Jars when, later on in their artistic evolution, they are manufactured with figurine heads on the stopper-caps: three are animal heads and the fourth is the odd (Masculine gender) one out featuring a male head. We see Egypt's legacy surely here as in the Old Testament and surviving as Christian iconography for the gospel writers. In Ezekiel 1:10 – "each living creature had 4 different faces" – 3 animal plus 1 male (human and/or angel) continued in religious consciousness to become accepted symbols for the gospel writers Matthew, Mark, Luke and John in illustrated medieval manuscripts until this day.

Figure 4

Figure 5

A legacy of sacred jars and cosmobiological associations can be discerned in two illustrations to the *Philosophia reformata* of Johann D. Mylius. Published in Frankfurt in 1622, they are considered the finest collection of alchemical engravings in existence. Figure 4 shows **3 + 1** ladies wearing Fixed Elements jars on their heads, they stand on circles containing the triangle glyphs for each of the four elements. Moreso in Figure 5, do we find a resemblance to Ancient Egypt ideas – the corner winds blow on to 4 jars in the register above the ecliptic. The ground register has **3 + 1** solar faced ladies pointing to their Cardinal mascots: 3 animals (ram, crayfish and goat) plus 1 different (a weighing-balance). The 4 tutelary Cardinal goddesses (Isis, Nephthys, Neith and Serket) have been associated with the zodiac Mutable signs organs (**3 + 1**) contained within Canopic Jars since the days of Queen Hetepheres, the mother of the builder of the Great Pyramid.

Transfer and Reversal

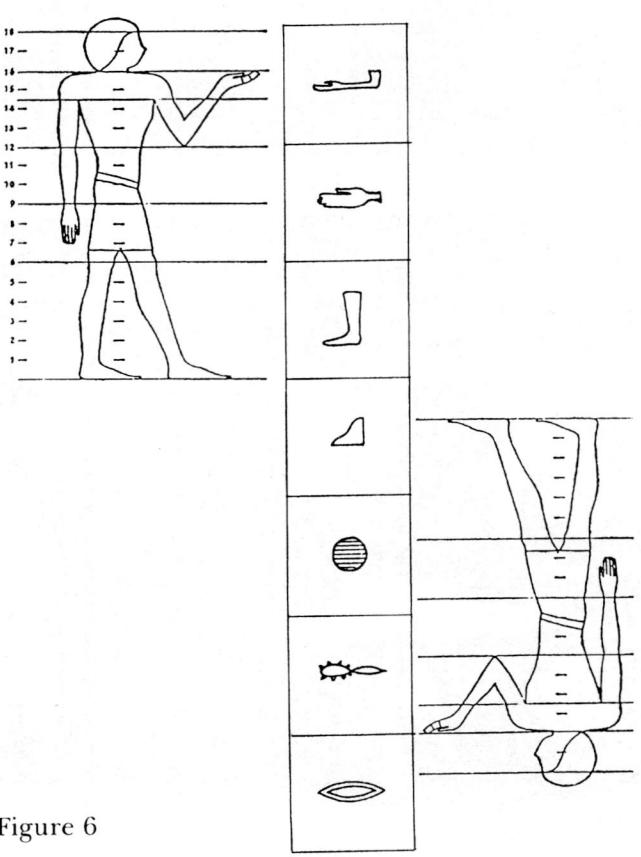

Figure 6

Look again at my (Figure 1) cryptogram diagram of 4 columns of hieroglyphs. The first column (Figure 6) may be taken as analogous to Man and Woman. There seems to be a corresponding ratio of the Old Kingdom Canon of Proportion to the zones for the *arm*, *hand* and *leg*. An inverted relationship can be gauged by placing the equidistant *mouth*, *teats* (!) and *placenta* up against a standard 18-square grid 'Canon of Man' with feet rather wittily walking towards the earth *hill* to climb. My conclusion from this juxtaposition is that below the lower horizon (the fearful 'upside down condition' the Egyptians so dreaded) lies the sublunary or hidden Feminine nature of 'Canon Man'.

The other columns are not so easy to explain and will be dealt with in another publication. Column 3 for instance, is interpreted by me as the celestial hemisphere (simply understated as the semicircular *bread-loaf*) which would be the cut-off point indicating the heavenly region of the northern Polar stars. The association of serpents with stellar phenomena is well-attested in religious writings from the Pyramid through to the Edfu Texts.

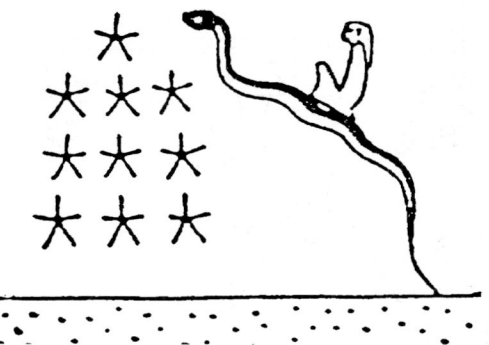

Shape and Geometry and the God Thoth

Can anything be made of the <u>shape</u> of the hieroglyphs-cryptogram? asks if anything can be made of the presentation? Can one see a similar geometric border outline in actual Egyptian art? A rectangle with 4 surplus elements jutting out from the corners brings to mind a vignette in the papyrus of Neskhonsu of the 21st Dynasty of "The Lake of Fire" (Figure 7,i). In this representation, the god Thoth, in his Earthly manifestation of Baboon, sits around a rectangular lake sectioned into 4 triangles. Viewed (Figure 7, ii) as a single quadrantic unit, the apex of each triangle spouts **Water** uppermost, with **Fire** insignia coming out from underneath the base which is guarded by creatures who walk the **Earth**. To ancient eyes, this apparently innocuous funerary art represents *Science*: - **3 + 1** Water, Earth and Fire with the sensible assumption of **Air** perceived as ambient. All this is several centuries before

Empedocles (490 – 430 BC), the acknowledged discoverer of the theory of the *elements*. The ancient alchemy gylph for "Air" (see Figure 4) is a triangle pointing up with a line through the upper third of the sign.

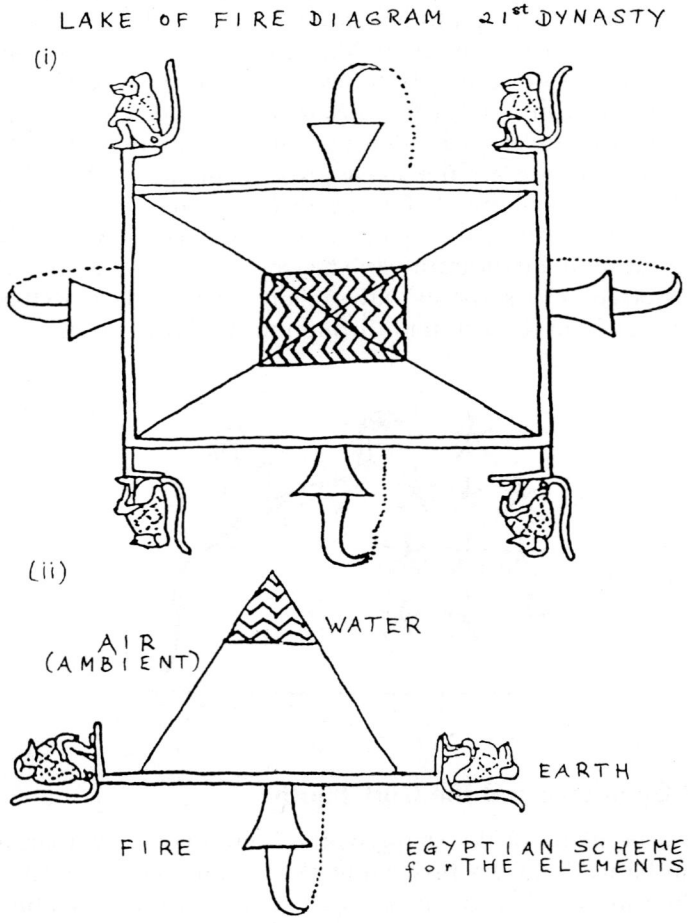

Figure 7

Thoth encrypted

Plato in his *Phaedrus* reveals that Thoth was the Egyptian god of wisdom, the original inventor of numbers, astronomy, and games of draughts and dice. However most importantly of all, Thoth was god of letters. In the absolute centre of my model cryptogram, the foundation letters of Egyptian hieroglyphs spell out the name **Dhwty** (see below), which is known phonetically to the Greeks as Thoth.

THOTH RULES, OKAY?

> *And Hermes Trismegistus is my name, because I possess the 3 parts of the wisdom of the whole world.*
>
> Zohar (written by Moses de Leon)

The first known appearance of Thoth seems to be in the Predynastic Period on the Ashmolean Museum fragment of the 'Battlefield Palette' as ibis-on-a-standard holding fast a foreign prisoner. His image is still true to form in reliefs of the 2nd Century AD in the catacombs of Kom es-Shoqafa at Alexandria (Figure 8), by which time Thoth is universally acknowledged to be Hermes by the Greeks and Mercury by the Romans. In his 2nd Century writings Plutarch (*On Isis and Osiris*, 12) narrates that Hermes once played a board game of draughs with the Moon, "winning from her the 70th part of each of her periods of illumination".

Figure 8.
A reconstruction of the last official version of Thoth in a 2ⁿᵈ Century AD Greco-Roman-Egyptian burial. The badly damaged scene in the Catacombs of Kom es-Shoqafa, Alexandria was discovered in 1993.

In the sacred Pyramid Texts, the god Thoth is always depicted ibis-on-a-standard, with no preceding hieroglyphs. During the building of the Pyramids, when hieroglyphs were at their most pristine level of accomplishment, much industry in quarrying and mining took place 225 km south east of Giza at Wadi Maghara in the Sinai where Thoth was worshiped locally. Here there are many impressive rock carvings dating from the 3ʳᵈ Dynasty showing kings smiting their ethnic enemies. One of the carvings shows Khufu, 4ᵗʰ Dynasty builder of the Great Pyramid knocking out the fallen captor before the familiar Thoth with ibis head on male torso, who holds a *was*-septre.

A tale of Mystery and Magic

A papyrus dating from the Hyksos period, written in classical Middle Egyptian and known as the Westcar Papyrus, contains stories set in the Old Kingdom. One notable tale describes how Khufu (the builder of the Great Pyramid) has spent time searching for the secret chambers of the sanctuary of Thoth to incorporate in his own temple. Djedi, the 110 years old magician, who is summoned by Khufu, only knows partial answers. Djedi tells Khufu that he does not know the number of secret chambers, but gives a cryptic location of Thoth's sanctuary. The riddle suggests that the location is at On, in the building called 'Inventory' in a chest of flint! This parable-tale sounds as if it has slipped in a reference to the long-lost "Hall of Records". On the assumption that Khufu did not succeed in solving Djedi's puzzle, it probably indicates that the secret depository of Thoth (and I would think '5' chambers!) will not be underneath his pyramid at Giza.

Building a Pyramid

Inspired by "Lake of Fire" drawings in papyri comprising joined triangles, the flat model can be overlaid with triangles – in fact, six of them (Figure 3). The two central triangles join together to form a square. The dividing line can only run one way otherwise it will bisect the 4 hieroglyphs of mound, quail-chick, bread and river. The diagram therefore has a left side and a right side. "Right" in Egyptian means "West" and "Left means "East and thus the dividing line is a **Meridian**. The 6 triangles may be placed over or made to form a pyramid, with the square underneath comprising two triangles hiding the 5-lettered name *Dḥwty* from view (Figure 9).

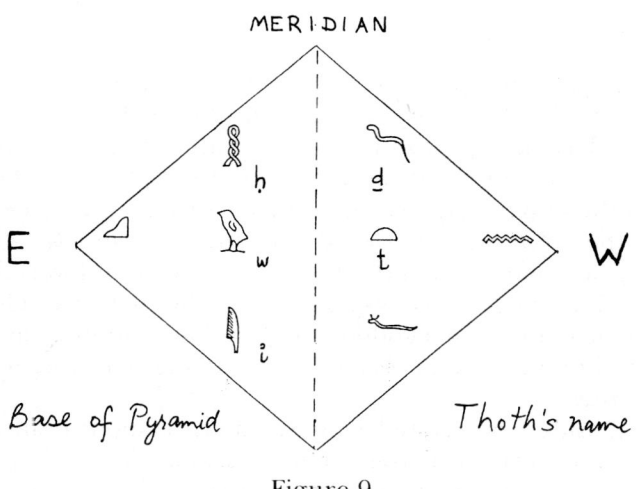

Figure 9

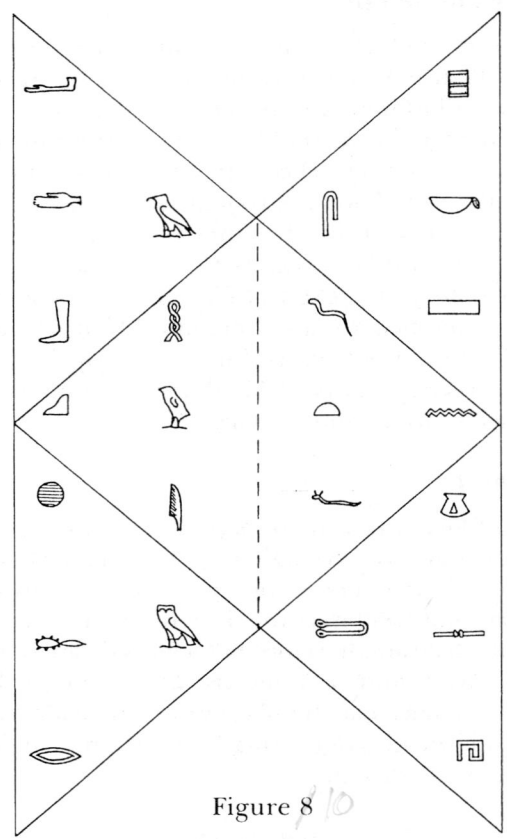

Figure 8

The 4 faces of the pyramid will be the North, South, East, and West aspects of the model (Figure 8). The North face (dedicated to the Cardinal goddess Neith) has hieroglyphs under the *owl* (the letter "M") which are face-value symbols of Nurture: the *mouth*, *teats* and the *placenta*. The South face (dedicated to the goddess Serket) has symbols that suggest material security: the *dwelling*, the *jar-stand*, the *door-bolt* and the *tethering rope*. The East face (dedicated to the goddess Nephthys) seems indicative of forceful action with the vulture (*Neophron percnopterus*), and limbs hieroglyphs. The West face (dedicated to the last Cardinal goddess Isis) might fancifully be associated with secondary wealth: the luxury *bolt of linen*, a dug-out *pool*, furniture and (shopping?) *basket*.

Leaving aside exaggerated modern interpretation of ancient symbols *per se*, we return to straight hieroglyphic translation. Astoundingly, the letters on the West wall spell out the name of the very sacred instrument (resembling a fish-tail in flint) the **pšš-k(f)** which is used in Opening of the Mouth ceremonies on the pharaoh's mummy.

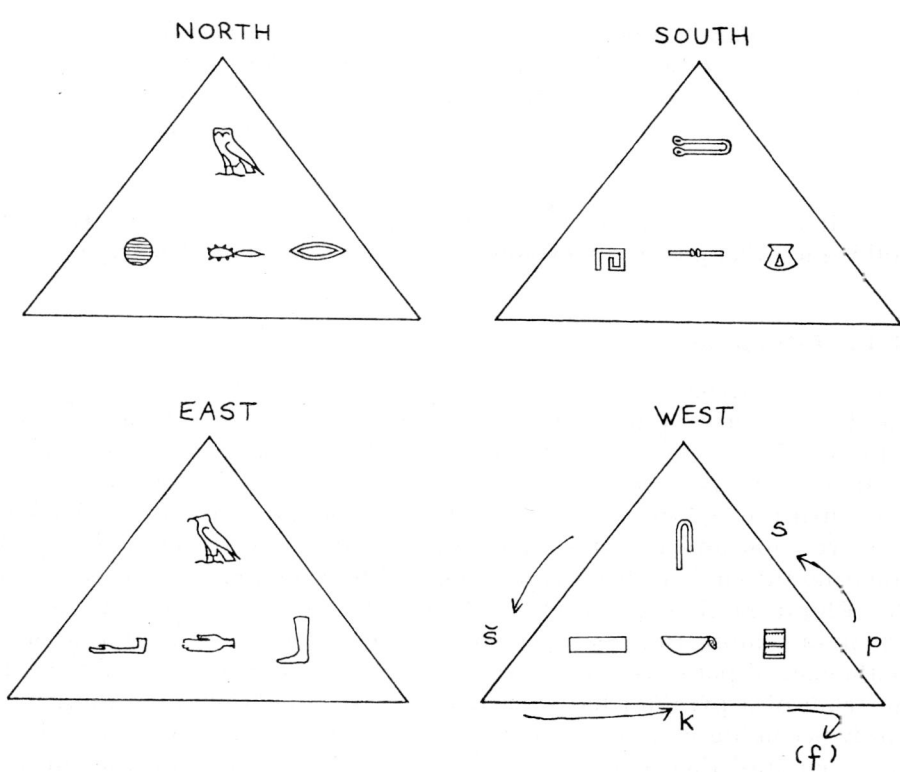

More Hidden Meanings?

Are there any other coded messages incorporating profound ideas or "truths" from the Pyramid Age? This seems very likely. Quite a lot of grouped hieroglyphs leap off the page indicating early disciplines of medicine (e.g. the Greek *Chymoi* – the "Humours"), astronomy and alchemy, as well as harmonics or even a diatonic scale for music – all of which ideas I would like to develop more fully later.

It is as well now to try out a more reductionist approach in ancient thinking terms which I hope will not conclude *reductio ad absurdum*. In a world without computer technology how would any **genius**, assigned the task of programming a large scale writing model representing all local natural philosophic knowledge for succeeding generations, tackle extra concepts of multiple dimensions or "virtual reality"? This end, in my opinion, was duly achieved but I remain in awe and at a loss to speculate when/how/by one or many/hieroglyphs were invented.

RA IS SUPREME

> *Make of man and woman a circle from that a square, then a triangle, then another circle, and you will have the Philosopher's Stone.*
> M. Maiier, 1618

It is said that Cosmology is the ultimate science since it deals with nothing less that the origin, evolution and fate of the entire Universe.

Going full circle

Obeying the dynamic principle in Egyptian art, its Canon of Proportion, the drawn hieroglyphs displayed throughout this article remain in intact grids, but I have allowed each of them the property of freely turning about on themselves. Another geometric mode in tune with Natural Philosophy is to turn the squares occupied by the hieroglyphs into circles. Back-to-front revision and reasoning have been *de rigueŕ* throughout this quest! Squaring the circle is dealt with in the Middle Kingdom papyrus known as the Rhind Mathematical (Nos. 41-43, 48, 50). One of the Ancient Egyptian's most impressive formulae recorded in this and another mathematical papyrus is the mysterious discovery that the volume of the frustrum of a pyramid has square section and faces of equal slope. It is slowly becoming more evident that mathematical sciences (e.g. knowledge of Pythagoras' theorem) existed within the Egyptian culture as an elite verbal tradition. The Greeks later plagiaristically catalogued rather than invented all that was known in previous superior cultures before their own rise to cultural supremacy.

The practical exercise of putting circles around the hieroglyphs (Fig. 10) housed in equally spaced squares turns out to be quite an occult discovery. The resulting astounding configuration of equal concentric circles is none other than a picture expression of profound cosmology ideas, generally attributed to the school of Aristotle, from which time the diagrams, assumed to accompany the teachings, have not survived.

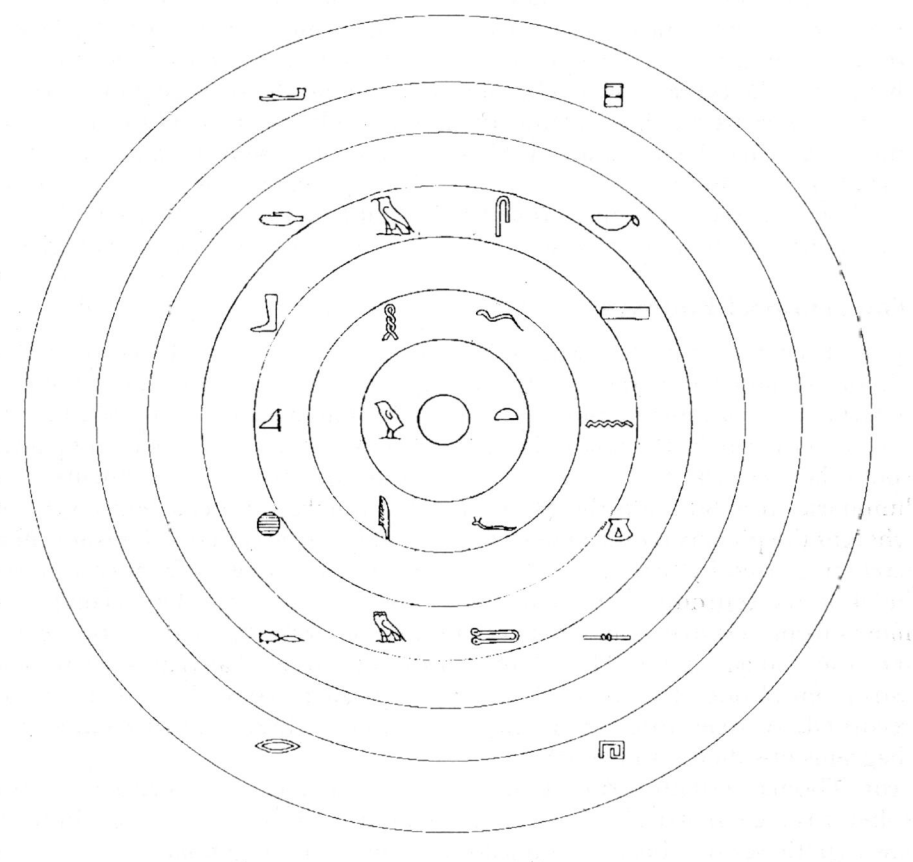

Figure 10

Invoking Aristotelian cosmology

Some two thousand years after the invention of hieroglyphs, Aristotle (384-322 BC) propounded his concentric cosmology whereby the Universe divided into a series of nested spheres containing the planets (Book 12, Chapter 8 *Metaphysics*). The "law" of Aristotelian cosmology is that a celestial orb rotates perpetually within a single space on the east-west axis and does not move from one place to another. My circular diagram for the 24 basic hieroglyphs fits well on to this concept. From the inner core (something akin to the centre of gravity perhaps), 7 spheres radiate. The theory lasted well into the Renaissance that rational knowledge ended at the outermost celestial sphere, where the mystery of God and creation began. Four hieroglyphs in the outermost sphere seem to say *hp* "law" and *re* "the god Ra" – the law of the sun god!

Plato (*Philebus*, 18d) remarks that "Thoth saw there existed a connection between the signs which lead to a Unity". This is more than likely the *Primum Mobile*, often discussed in medieval and Renaissance manuscripts, the vital force that moves the celestial orbs. The rings drawn onto the hieroglyph pattern are highly suggestive of the 7 planetary spheres with assumed orbits of the sun, moon, Mercury, Venus, Mars, Jupiter and Saturn – similar diagrams were a regular feature in medieval iconography. During the day, the moon is invisible, which would account in an emphatic Solar-cult-Egyptian belief system, that this model turns out to have the space immediately below the sun void of hieroglyphs!

The genius of Eudoxos

Aristotle cites the vanished work of Eudoxos (408 - 355 BC) of Knidos (in Asia Minor – modern Turkey) who was a generation before him. Eudoxos described 7 concentric spheres with the common centre representing the centre of the earth. He believed that the motion of the Sun, Moon and planets could be accounted for by a combination of circular movements. The luminaries (the Sun and the Moon) needed to take up 3 concentric spheres, whereas the planets required in each case 4 concentric spheres. The outermost circle (reported by Aristotle and also by Simplicius) moving from east to west in 24 hours, reproduces the daily motion of the fixed stars. The second circle moves from west to east about an axis perpendicular to the plane of the ecliptic (i.e. the zodiac circle). The oldest illustrated Greek papyrus known is an astronomical one. This is the Letronne papyrus (now in the Louvre) which recorded, two centuries later, the discoveries of Eudoxos with some early diagrams of spheres and zodiac.

Ivor Thomas (1939) writes that Eudoxos's system of concentric rotating spheres is a geometrical *tour de force*: "in all of the history of science there are few hypotheses that bear so unmistakably the stamp of **genius**".

The Tether at the Centre of the Zodiac

This system of genius was used for working out the longitude, the stationary points and the retrograde motions of Jupiter, Saturn and Mercury – the first attempt to explain the apparent irregularities of planetary movement. Within the rings of the planets is some kind of "spherical lemniscate" which Eudoxos calls a *hippopede* (or horse-fetter) Not forgetting that horses were unknown in Egypt when hieroglyphs were invented, is just a happy coincidence that, in the middle ring of my concentric circles, appears the Egyptian animal tethering-rope?

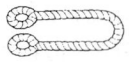

A very rare token and small piece of archaic Greek art meeting non-conformist Egyptian art (Figure 11ii) is to be found on a 26th Dynasty sailor's coffin. The Greco-Egyptian *Hippocampus* (the stomach-less and viviparous sea horse) on the register facing the Cardinal (also birth) goddesses Isis and Nephthys was described by Margaret Murray (see HISTORICAL STUDIES, 1911, 39-40, pl XXI).

In the middle sphere of Figure 10 (matching the middle spheres of Eudoxos' *hippopede*) you will find the Egyptian hippopotamus or cattle-fetter – "ṯ" in transliteration, together with the 7 other hieroglyphs: m $ḫ$ g b $š$ 3 and $ꜣ$. The temptation to experiment with anagrams is too great I hope you will agree!

$Ḥ$ 3 b is the word for Hippo, and $š$ s is the word for rope or cord.

The Hippopotamus is know as a Constellation in Egyptian astronomy (see Kurt Locher in ARCHAEOSTRONOMY, no.9 [JHA,xvi,] 1985).

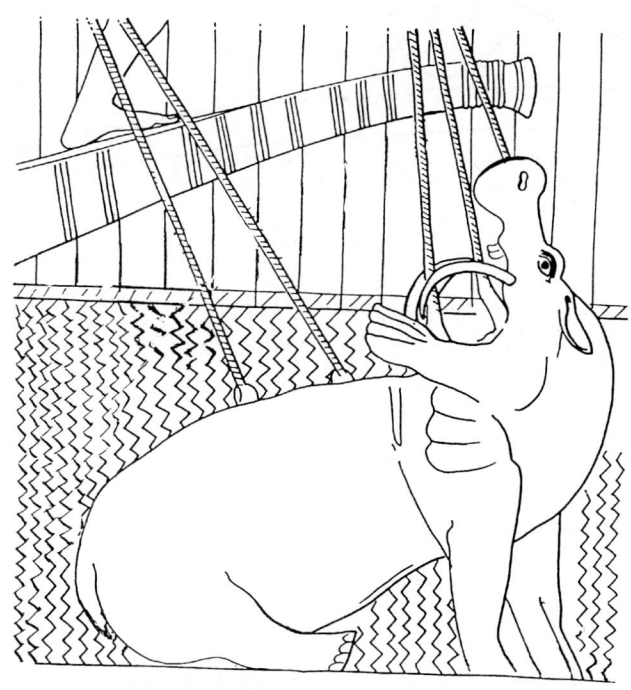

Figure 11
(i)

Hippo-fetters!
After the 5th Dynasty tomb of Ti at Saqqara

Figure 11 /2
(ii)
*Greek Art meets Egyptian Art approx. 590 BC
The Goddess Isis and Hippocampus on 26th Dynasty
sailor's coffin.*
Author's own sketch

Another arrangement of the letters:

G s 3   M s ḫ ṯ b

Msḫ tyw is the Constellation "Foreleg" or Ursa Major, *ṯb* in Gardiner is taken to mean "shod". Taking an obvious clue from the Greek "pede", *Msḫ-ṯb* would indicate the shoe or hoof of the Foreleg. Might it therefore be translated. "The tilt (or slant) of the part where Ursa Major is shod"? On a star map, this locates as the binary stars Mizar and Alcor which are the best known double stars visible to the naked eye in the Great Bear constellation. Any number of professional star watchers in antiquity would have noted over the years the wobbling effect which tells of a companion star. So the anagram message of *gs3 Msh̬-tb* could be strongly interpreted as: "the wobbling (rather than 'tilting') motion of the binary star Mizar".

No matter what, my final anagram:

$$g\ m\ \underline{h}\ s\ b\ 3\ \check{s}\ \underline{t}$$

can certainly be read out as "Look at stars secret"!

The major doctrine of Egyptian cosmology whereby Ra brought everything into a state of being with his one-handed copulation (note where the hand "**d**" and the vulture *3* = the Egyptian word "to copulate" lie in the circled diagram) is coincidentally close to some recent advanced thinking in prebiotic chemistry. See CHEMICAL COMMUNICATIONS 1996 (p2627) for theory of an extraterrestrial origin for the one-handedness of the chemistry of life. We are told by boffins that neutron stars throw out electromagnetic radiation that is circularly polarised (**chiral** radiation) anticlockwise from the star's northern hemisphere, and clockwise from the southern hemisphere (NEW SCIENTIST, January 1997).

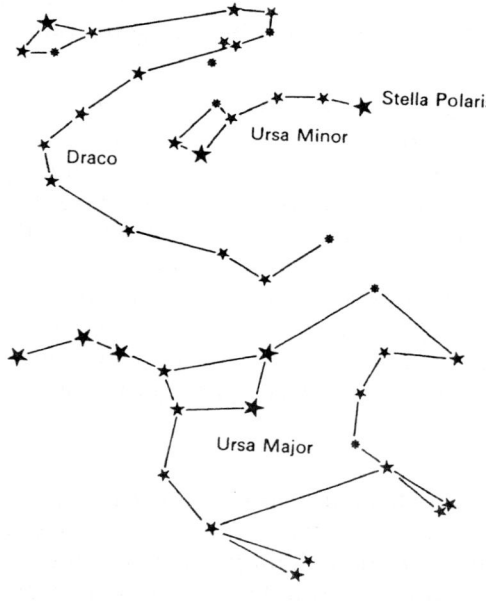

LOOSE ENDS

> *When I met with the divine and venerable theory of the heavens, I wished to purge my character of all evil and all stain and form a conception in advance of the soul as immortal.*
> Vettius Valens, *The Anthology Book* VI
> 2nd Century AD

Codes

The earliest explicit use of a secondary layer of meaning embedded in plaintext, is reputed to have been favoured by the ancient Israelites. A 1st Century kabbalist, Nechunya ben HaKanah, claimed that the name of God was a key to the times and seasons as well as the time-scale between the origin of the Universe and the creation of mankind. In a sensational book on the Bible Code, Jeffrey Satinover (1997) says that the Hebrew letters for B,H,R,D represented a hidden number from which the lunar month important for the religious calendar could be calculated. The Egyptian equivalent of these letters happen to be grouped together in the upper left-hand quadrant of my diagram (Fig 1). This is possibly another 3 + 1 example: three letters B, H, D group with the transliteral letter "ā" which gives the phonetic "R" sound.

Games

There is a connection between board games (mentioned earlier) and the calendar. By far the most popular and enduring throughout Pharaonic history was the game *Senet*. A late Roman period papyrus fragment from Oxyrynchus describes the traditional 30 squares on the board as the days in a **Lunar** month. Furthermore, the schematic Egyptian Lunar year of 360 days is obtained by adding the numbers of the last 15 squares (see Kendall, 1978). It must now be radiantly obvious, if we recall Hesyra's circular diagram that, with its Solar attached gaming pieces of lions and globes, the Old Kingdom game of *Mḫn* was originally modelled on the path of the **Sun**.

Holy writing

Throughout their extraordinary history, the Egyptians were precise about recording stars' movements and vital Nile water levels, as well as mundane measurement of land, and the weighing of precious metals and body parts too (at autopsy). Thoth was the patron deity of all these levels of scribal activities. Commercially, the usefulness of writing, by virtue of efficiency-factor, had to be a major contribution towards the achievement of continual mega-scale building projects, the success of which Ancient Egypt's fame rests.

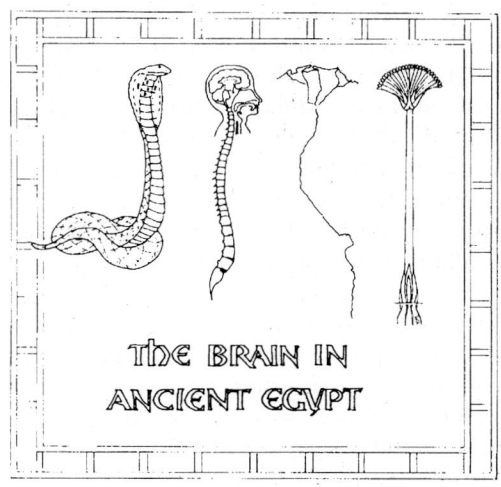

THE BRAIN IN ANCIENT EGYPT

Even to the extent of mummification, the wily Ancient Egyptians went to extraordinary lengths to hide their brain-power. Since my degree essay (1994), I have objected to the widely held assumption that the Egyptian embalmers must have thrown away the brain. Herodotus (Book II, 86-8) tells how the *perfect* removal of the brain uses an *iron* hook (not flint, copper, or reed instruments which could do the procedure equally as well). The head has long had a stellar association with the first Cardinal sign Aries and the Egyptian goddess of this region, Nephthys, shares a linking association with the metal iron. Later in alchemy, the metal iron belongs to the god Mars who wields rulership over the zodiacal sign Aries.

Three texts in the New Kingdom *Book of the Dead* convince me that the hacked-up-brain mess was dropped into (the element of Aries) **Fire** (see Spell 82). Spell 15 ends with "**Thoth** has consigned him to the knife; he has made him non-existent". In Spell 94, the scribe requests his writing-kit of water-bowl, palette and "the putrid effluent of Osiris" with which to carry on his sacred writing. The brain, in my opinion, was purified at death in fire (possibly an incense-burner) and the soot residue was mixed into the scribes black ink – thus giving a recycle treatment for the holier-than-thou **hieroglyphs**!

Back to the End

This enquiry had dealt in an intriguing way with a fractional tip of the iceberg, or rather, with the apex of a pyramid. By the Middle Kingdom, when Egyptian writing had attained its pure peak, there were **24 x 31** hieroglyphic signs more or less in constant use, and they remained fundamentally unchanged until the Greeks occupied Egypt. The Prime number **31** was remarked by Flinders Petrie (1911) when commenting on the Harris Papyrus (reign of Ramses III) "it has often been noticed that in sections which refer to offerings of 31 years, the number 31 and its multiples often occur". I hope that I have shown that many more things allied to the simple basic hieroglyphs still need in depth exploration.

In the 21st century, up-dated knowledge of Ancient Egypt will move along with cyber-world rapidity to help elucidate language problems. We owe those anonymous great minded people, before the advent of the individual Greek celebrity, a debt of gratitude for pioneer work in 'sciences' for their times. These achievements are all too often ignored or played down by the non-scientifically trained Classical arts scholars who prefer to steer away from what they perceive as realms of fancy. Many an amused departed Egyptian soul might wince in his mummy wrappings when his technical attributions and proud poster displays are labelled "magic".

Well over 5,000 years ago, Fathers of Science - the unknown Egyptian Newtons and Keplers - hid in playful and spectacular ways vast quantities of the equivalent of their higher-degree course knowledge., Some of these guaranteed to please hiding places provide immeasurable delight in lieu of apology for secreting away profound truths before the observer's very eyes. Included amongst enchanted hiding places are the more accessible hieroglyphic alphabet, board games and idyllic tomb scenes.

Lulled into a false sense of what-you-see-is-what-you-get, the euphoric laden and spellbound lovers of Ancient Egypt, seem to be permanently seduced by the charm, warmth and innocence of the visible arts falsifying the natural world. Surely a clever ruse to blind the observer to advanced rational ideas such as mathematical formulae on the earliest offering tables, or related(Figure 12) astronomical phenomena (eclipses, stations, solstices and equinoxes) hidden amongst ethereal characters in scenes like "Hunting in the Marshes" (Figure 13).

Figure 13
*Author's sketch showing 3 + 1 means (3 cords plus 1
sharp harpoon) of having power over changeable stellar
forces from the safety of the dependable Solar vessel.*

Long may the dream continue, but for those who want insights from the statistical minority in Ancient Egypt with extremely high I.Qs., it is time to brush aside their cover of naive façade and pay homage to the Spirits of those multiple talents emanating from true genius behind the invention of hieroglyphs.

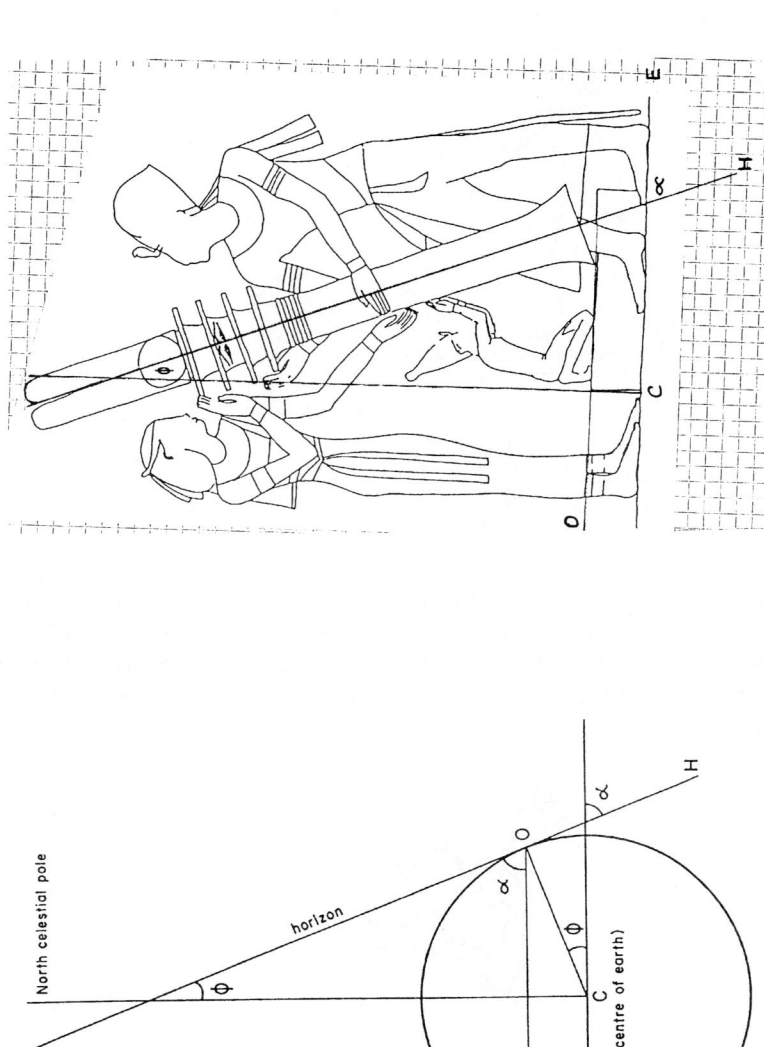

Figure 12
Diagrams of the same principles demonstrating the angles formed by the intersection of the terrestrial equator and the North – South axis with the horizon.
Left – Greek astronomical geometry (after D.R. Dicks, 1970)
Right – Egyptian (after Seti I, 19th Dynasty) equinoctial instrumentation using the **Djed** tilting-dioptra.

THE END

SELECTIVE BIBLIOGRAPHY

Baines, J (1989) Communication and Display: The Integration of Early Egyptian Art and Writing, Antiquity 63, 471-482.

Blackman, A. (1988) The Story of King Kheops and the Magicians transcribed from Papyrus Westcar (Berlin Papyrus 3033), Reading.

Brewer, D. & Friedman, R. (1989) Fish and Fishing in Ancient Egypt, Warminster.

David, M. (1965) Le Débat sur les ecritures et l'hiéroglyphe aux XVIIe et XVIIIe siècles, et l'application de la notion de déchiffrement aux écritures mortes, Paris.

Davis, W. (1979) Plato on Egyptian Art, JEA 65, 121-7.

Fairservis, W. (1983) Hierakonpolis– The Graffiti and the Origins of Egyptian Hieroglyphic Writing, Anthropology 2, New York.

Gardiner, A. (1915) JEA 2, 74.
- (1957) Egyptian Grammar, Oxford.

Iversen, E. (1993) The Myth of Egypt and Its Hieroglyphs in European Tradition, Princeton.

Kendall, T. (1978) Passing through the Netherworld the meaning and play of Senet, an ancient Egyptian funerary game, Boston.

Kirk, G., Raven, J. & Schofield, M. (1983) The Presocratic Philosophers, Cambridge.

Lesko, L. (1994) Pharaoh's Workers, the Villagers of Deir el Medina, Cornell.

Murray, M. (1951) The Splendour that was Egypt, London.

Petrie, W. (1912) Formation of the Alphabet, London.

Robins, G. & Shute, C. (1987) The Rhind Mathematical Papyrus, an ancient Egyptian text, London.

Satinover, J. (1997) The Truth behind the Bible Code, London.

Thomas, I. (1991) Greek Mathematical Works I Thales to Euclid, Harvard.

Weitzmann, K. (1970) Illustrations in Roll and Codex, Princeton.
- (1971) The Greek Sources of Islamic Scientific Illustrations. In: Studies in Classical and Byzantine Manuscript Illumination, 20-44. Ed. Kessler, H., Chicago.